Sky Pony Press books may be purchased in bulk at special discounts for sales promotion, corporate gifts, fund-raising, or educational purposes. Special editions can also be created to specifications. For details, contact the Special Sales Department, Sky Pony Press, 307 West 36th Street, 11th Floor, New York, NY 10018 or info@skyhorsepublishing.com.

Sky Pony® is a registered trademark of Skyhorse Publishing, Inc.®, a Delaware corporation.

Visit our website at www.skyponypress.com.

10 9 8 7 6 5 4 3 2 1

Manufactured in China, September 2022
This product conforms to CPSIA 2008

Library of Congress Cataloging-in-Publication Data is available on file.

Cover design by Elke Kohlmann & Kai Texel
Cover illustrations by Dagmar Geisler
US Edition edited by Nicole Frail

Print ISBN: 978-1-5107-7135-2
Ebook ISBN: 978-1-5107-7311-0

If My Parents Are Divorced

How to Talk about Separation, Divorce, and Breakups

Written and
Illustrated by
Dagmar Geisler

Translated by
Andy Jones Berasaluce

Sky Pony Press
New York

Something is different today.

Everyone's having fun kneading clay, but Marie looks strange the whole time. She hasn't even started.

"What's up with you?" asks Tom.

"With me, nothing at all," says Marie. "It has to do with Rosalie and Flo. Those are our neighbors' kids. Rosalie's my friend."

"What's wrong with them?" Felix asks.

Marie lets out a huge sigh. "Rosalie told me yesterday that her parents are separating."

"Separating?" Jana asks.

"They're getting divorced," explains Owen.

It's true, though. Sometimes parents break up. It hurts, and it makes no difference whether they're married or simply live together with their family.

When married people split up, divorce usually follows. When getting married, a couple signs a piece of paper that says they want to be married. Then they receive a marriage certificate that makes it a legal union.

When getting divorced, they must sign papers again, this time saying they want to separate. And then a great many other things have to be settled.

Things like money and the house and, sometimes, who takes care of the children.

It is very hard for some children to understand how and why their parents are splitting up.

How is it possible that the love between two parents just goes away?

It doesn't happen just like that. It may take a while before parents admit that they may no longer be as good of a match as they thought they'd be at the beginning of their relationship.

Believe it or not, there was once a time when all of our parents didn't even know each other. They may have traveled the world and didn't even know the other existed.

Mom

TapTapTap

Taptaptap

Taptaptap

They didn't know they would one day meet, and they certainly didn't know they'd start a family together.

Here's where they almost met . . .

Here too

TapTapTap

This may seem strange to you, because when you were born, they already knew each other and were already your parents.

There is, by the way, a difference between the love parents have for each other, and the love parents have for their children.

The relationship between two grown-ups may come to an end. But the bond between parents and their children always remains.

In both cases, the word *love* is used, which may lead to confusion. If there were different words for the feeling parents have for each other and the feeling parents have for their children, you would immediately realize that these are two very different things. These are different kinds of love.

Taptaptap

Taptaptap

Parents and their children belong together from the beginning. No one can break up this love.

← Dad

Taptaptap

Marie tells the others what she found out from Rosalie. Tom also knows quite a bit about what happens with adults when they are about to break up. Some time ago, he experienced it himself, as did Emma.

Sometimes they cry . . .

Even the cat notices that something's not right.

. . . sometimes they just sit there . . .

. . . sometimes
they fight . . .

. . . or they don't
talk to each
other at all . . .

. . . sometimes one of
them drives away
suddenly . . .

. . . sometimes they are
completely done with the
relationship . . . and . . .
and . . .

Oh dear! My parents often argue. What if they get divorced, too?
But your parents also show affection sometimes when they pick you up.

Other children know this fear, too. But parents don't split up just because they argue sometimes. Arguing is normal and happens in general, no matter how much you love each other.

When separating, there may be more reason to argue, but arguing is not the reason for separation.

Precisely! They love each other!

When a separation occurs, it's not easy for anyone. The adults had wished that their love would last forever. They're sad that it wasn't meant to be. Or they're angry. Maybe they blame each other, too. In any case, there are a great many feelings that are new to the adults, as well. They're busy almost all the time and may not pay as much attention to their children as they usually do.

Children sometimes think that they can do something to make everything better. But they can't. This is an adult matter; children can't do anything about it. It's not their responsibility.

I really wanted to make myself invisible.

I thought if I behaved better, then maybe everything would be fine again.

Some kids are especially "difficult" during this time. Maybe they think that their parents will forget, with all the fuss they create, that they wanted to split up.

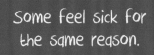

Some feel sick for the same reason.

At first, I thought it was all happening because of me. It was somehow my fault.

Many children are in the same situation as Emma. It's such a strange feeling. It feels like you did something. But you didn't do anything that made your parents think of separating.

As said before:

This is not the children's responsibility, and they aren't at fault.

Children do not need to keep these feelings to themselves. It's good to talk to someone about it. You always have the right to ask for help. Or just to talk to someone you trust about what moves you or what scares you. This is especially true, of course, during difficult times like these.

Dad and I live in the yellow house

The old tractor belongs to Harry. That's our neighbor.

When I get my driver's license, then I can drive it, too.

There comes a time when the difficult start to a divorce is finally over. Once the adults know how they want to live after separating, it gets easier.

Country Box

With Mom, I live right above the ice cream parlor.

Louis lives next door

Ice Cream Palace

My favorite flavors: Vanilla, Mango, Apricot, Caramel.

Louis and I are currently inventing an elevator machine for ice cream scoops.

Sometimes something new happens that can even be really nice. Tom now has two bedrooms: one at his father's in the country and one at his mother's in the city.

City Box

For Emma, several things have changed, too. She still lives with her mother in the same house, but they do a great deal of things differently. And every two weeks, she goes to see her father for a few days.

At Daddy's, I also have a bedroom. It's tiny but very comfy.

Tom likes the way it is now. Mom and Dad are much happier than they were before the separation. And he feels equally good in each of his new homes.

He only gets that guilty feeling sometimes.

For example, after he gets something nice from Mom or after he goes on a trip with Dad.

How was it?

Not bad . . .

Should he tell Dad about the gift from Mom? Or should he tell Mom how awesome the trip with Dad was? What if the two are still a little bit sour about each other?

But actually, this is something Tom doesn't have to worry about. After all, if parents don't get along so well, that's their concern. Children can love their mothers, and children can love their fathers. This also means that children can be happy about everything they experience with each of them. Or sometimes can be angry with each of them.

Everyone, big or small, is allowed to have their own feelings.

Even if two parents can no longer get along, they can know that their child loves both of them.

The children in class have been talking for a while now, only Felix hasn't said a word.

"What's up with you?" asks Owen.

Felix opens his mouth a couple times and then closes it again. A little while later, he starts talking.

"My parents want to separate, too. They're planning to tell me today. I didn't want to spy, but I heard them when I had to go to the bathroom." He speaks quickly, but the others understand him anyway.

It's not easy to find a way to start talking about these things. Sometimes you may also feel that if you don't talk about what's bothering you, it's not real or true.

But now that it's out, Felix feels a little lighter. And that's good. Also, Emma can now explain wish lists to him.

Wish lists are really a good idea.

They helped Emma when her parents separated. She tells Felix that he should draw or write two of them. On the first wish list goes all the wishes that come to mind. Even those that may never come true. It does you good and helps you get to know yourself and your feelings a little better.

The first wish list is strictly secret! Not for the public.

I want Mom + Dad to stay together

That's my wish.

I'll let them out as soon as they make up!

I'll take them as prisoners on a trip around the world!

The second wish list is for what can help here and now to cope a little better with the situation.

Right away, Felix gets a good idea.

The second wish list is intended for your parents.

When you have to ~~eng~~ argue, I want to go to Grandma's and bake a cake. You can have a piece when you pick me up.

With chocolate + raisins

Advice and Help

Children's Rights Council
Phone: (800) 304-3107
www.crckids.org

Dads Resource Center
19 Colonnade Way Ste 117 #190
State College, PA 16803
Phone: (833) 323-7748
Email: info@dadsrc.org
https://dadsrc.org

Divorce and Children
Email: christinamcghee@divorceandchildren.com
https://divorceandchildren.com

Divorce Care
Phone: (800) 489-7778
Email: info@divorcecare.org
https://divorcecare.org

Divorce Magazine
2255B Queen St. East, Suite #1179
Toronto, ON M4E 1G3
Canada
Phone: (866) 803-6667
Email: catherine@divorcemarketinggroup.com
https://divorcemag.com

Help Guide
1250 6th Street, Suite 201
Santa Monica, CA 90401
https://www.helpguide.org/.../children-and-divorce.htm

I Am a Child of Divorce
Email: wayne@iamachildofdivorce.com
https://iamachildofdivorce.com

Nationwide Children's Hospital
700 Childrens Drive
Columbus, OH 43205
Phone: (614) 722-2000
Email: CommunityRelations@Nationwide Childrens.org
https://nationwidechildrens.org

Sesame Street in Communities
1900 Broadway (One Lincoln Plaza)
New York, NY 10023
Email: Communities@sesame.org
https://sesamestreetincommunities.org/topics/divorce/

Woman's Divorce
624 Commerce Way, PMB 127
Clovis, NM 88101
https://womansdivorce.com

This concerns everyone!

Good news first. The number of divorces continues to decline. A positive trend, I think. Nonetheless, in Germany, where this author lives, between 130,000 and 200,000 children are directly affected annually by their parents separating. This is not just an issue for those directly involved, though.

I'd like to see a culture of conversation regarding separation and divorce that enables one to speak about this topic objectively and without fear. An open approach can help children speak sooner about their worries and needs.

They may feel stuck to some extent at first, but they will later be led into and supported during the new phase of life that follows a possible separation.

Perhaps they'll then also dare to speak of their own wishes regarding this future.

Surely you know the African proverb: "It takes a village to raise a child."

For me, that also means: A child is never alone with their problems. The community that surrounds the child, be it daycare, school, or friends, helps with getting through tough times well. Every good conversation is an important building block.

If I can contribute to that with this book, I would be delighted.

Dagmar Geisler

Dagmar Geisler has already supported several generations of parents in accompanying their children through emotionally difficult situations. With her picture book series Safe Child, Happy Parent, the author and illustrator sensitively deals with the most important topics related to growing up: from body awareness to exploring one's own emotional world to social interaction. Her work always includes a helping of humor, especially when things get serious. Her books have been translated into twenty languages and published around the world.

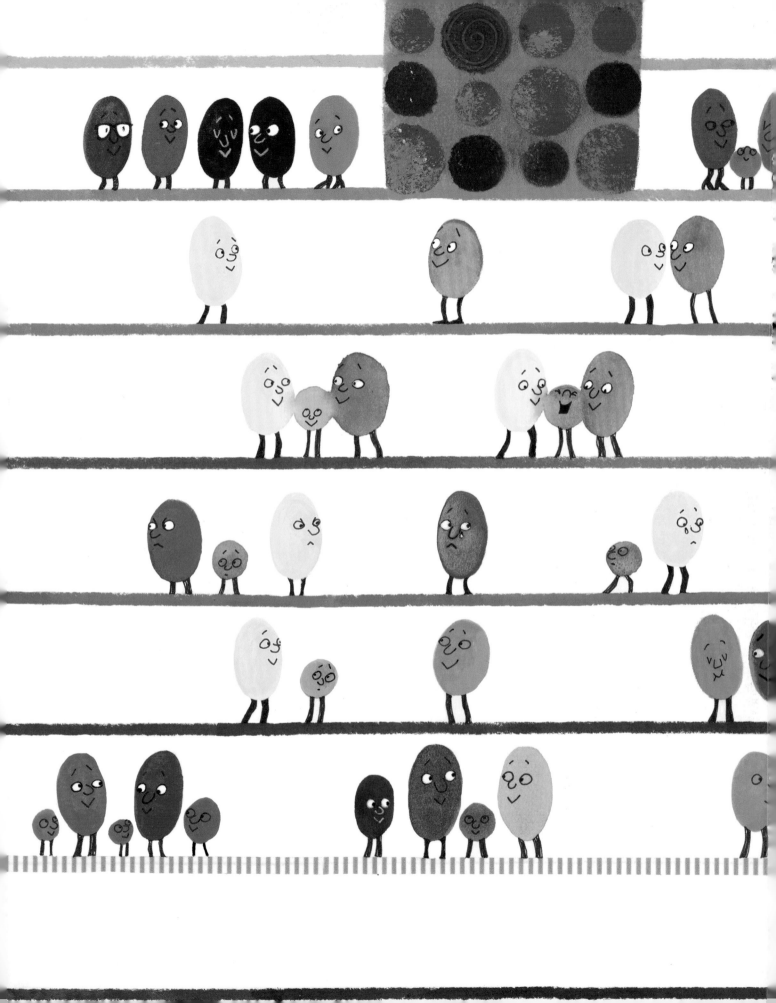